INSPIRATIONS

POEMS OF
LIFE AND LOVE

KATHRYN CAROLE ELLISON

Published by Lady Bug Books, an imprint of Brisance Books Group.
Lady Bug Press and the distinctive ladybug logo are registered trademarks of
Lady Bug Books, LLC.

Lady Bug Books
400 112th Avenue N.E.
Suite 230
Bellevue, WA   98004
www.ladybugbooks.com

For information about custom editions, special sales and permissions, please contact
Brisance Books Group at specialsales@brisancebooksgroup.com

Manufactured in the United States of America
ISBN: 978-1-944194-07-9

First Edition: May 2016

A NOTE FROM THE AUTHOR

The poems in this book were written over many, many years...
as gifts, of sorts, to my children. I began writing them in the
1970s, when my children were reaching the age of reason and
as I found myself in the position of becoming a single parent.
I needed something special to share with them—something that
would become a tradition, a ritual they could always count on...

And so the Advent Poems began—one day, decades ago—
with a poem 'gifted' to them each day during the December
holiday season every year. The poems were accompanied by a
little trinket or sweet for them to enjoy. Forty years later... my
children still look forward to the poems that started a family
tradition that new generations have come to cherish.
(Or is it the trinkets they love?)

It's my sincere hope that you will embrace and enjoy them
as we have and share them with those you love.

Children of the Light was among the first poems I wrote and
is included in each of my *Poems of Life and Love* books:
Heartstrings, Inspirations, and *Celebrations.* After writing
hundreds of poems, it is still my favorite. The words came
from my heart and my soul and flowed so effortlessly that it
was written in a single sitting. All I needed to do was capture
the words on paper. *Light,* to me, represented all that was
good and pure and right with the world, and I believed then—
as I do today—that those elements live in my children...
and perhaps in all of us. We need only to dare...

DEDICATION

To my parents: Herb and Bernice Haas

Mom, you were the poet who went before me...
unpublished, but appreciated nonetheless.

And Dad, you always believed in me,
no matter what direction my life took.
Thank you for your faith in me,
and for your unconditional love.

TABLE OF CONTENTS

LIFE'S JOYS

LIFE'S LESSONS

LIFE'S GIFTS

LIFE'S JOYS

SILENCE

Watch the rain – it always stops.
And that's true for thunder as well.
No natural outpouring goes on and on,
So speak briefly if you've something to tell.

A leader teaches more through being than
Through doing; his glibness to quell.
The quality of one's silence tells more, by far,
Than the casting of one's verbal spell.

Be still and follow your inner wisdom.
To know it you have to be still.
Your words carry weight when they're deeply felt;
They also carry good will.

When leading others, sincerity counts;
It guarantees effective skill.
When you're in touch with your own true Source
You consciously cooperate at will.

When you work hand in hand with your Source
Your effectiveness has great appeal;
But if you are only playing a game
Your motives you can't conceal.

Remember that the method is
An awareness-of-process deal.
Reflect. Be still. Be true to yourself.
What do you deeply feel?

DARE TO SOAR

What would you attempt to do
If you knew you could not fail?
If all restraints were taken away
How high would you dare to scale?

If all your needs were met and you
Were free to follow your dream,
How far would you go, and what would you do?
Just what would be your theme?

The fear we place on failure can be
What holds us back from glory.
We worry what others might think of us –
We heed the derogatory.

So, failure is but an attitude, and
It doesn't exist at all.
No matter how high you choose to climb
It's impossible for you to fall.

HAPPINESS

There is no way to happiness.
Happiness is the way.
Those words will bring you great success
Today, and every day.

No need to wait for another "throb"
To make you happy – no more!
Happiness is an inside job,
Effervescing from the core.

It comes to you when wise choices are made,
And from owning your inner talk.
Make sure the messages that are relayed
Are aligned when you walk your walk.

ATTITUDE IS THE KEY

Attitude is the key, it's said,
And yours is good, my dears.
You're free from debilitating thoughts
That bring on senseless fears.

You're learning to be responsible
For your own thoughts and actions.
You know that whatever happens
Results from your own life transactions.

You create for yourself whatever you need
In honing your ability for seeing.
As an internal person you draw on the power
That resides within your own being.

You can observe others with open eyes;
You can see their struggles, and learn.
You then can draw on your internal powers
To choose with enhanced skill to discern.

I see you learning to trust yourselves.
Like anything else, it takes rehearsal.
Practice the trust; it's so important,
And don't worry if there's some reversal.

You're human, you know. Isn't that grand?
Some days you're stronger or weaker.
Keep the percentages high for self-trust,
And continue to be the seeker.

Just know I love you with all my heart,
And I trust that God's plan for you
Will provide exactly what you need to grow
Into the very, very best TWO.

You're unique to you and very special to me.
Sometimes I ask, "Is it true?
That God chose me to share your lives?"
Just know that I love you.

HIGH IDEALS

Ideals are like stars, you will not succeed
In touching them with your hands.
But they will guide you on your way
As you cross life's shifting sands.

Ideals direct destiny, they're the basis for character,
The motive for achievement overall.
They won't let you settle for the lows in life.
They'll make sure you always walk tall.

Ideals won't let you make a truce
With evil; they'll keep you straight.
They are the power to fashion and shape your lives.
Your integrity determines your fate.

Ideals are the blueprint of higher living.
Set your goals, and aim for the heights!
With high ideals you can't go wrong.
Love life! Take great big bites!

Whether you reach the top, or not,
With high ideals you still win.
Ideals keep you striving; they give you power
Which you need in order to begin.

Ideals are the urging of the better self.
They make you what you are, inside.
They give you courage to meet life head on.
They won't let you run and hide.

KINDNESS

When you show kindness, it's very much
Like planting a seed in the ground.
The fruit is usually not harvested
Until later, when you're not around.

Too often we fail to recognize
That the power of a touch is profound;
And a listening ear, a kind word here and there
Could turn another's life around.

Have you noticed that from gentle people,
A quiet strength often comes from within?
It acts as a magnet, drawing you close
Until, almost magically, calmness sets in.

Kindness has converted more sinners than zeal,
Eloquence and learning combined.
Kindness is the golden chain
That joins together all of mankind.

Let kindness be the path you take,
And take it without delay.
Opt for a bit more than might be needed –
You'll reap your rewards every day.

Remember to treat other people
In a manner that does disarm.
Kindness is the coat you wear
To keep others in your life warm.

YOUR LIFE

Your main task in life is to give birth to yourself;
To become all you can possibly be.

The most important product of your effort
Is your own unique personality!

Cheerfulness

"Wondrous is the strength of cheerfulness,"
Said one Thomas Carlyle one day.
He claimed that cheerful people
Could accomplish more with a happy way.

Not only accomplish more, he insisted,
But better, and without delay
Than people who are sad and sullen.
(The sad ones reek "doomsday!")

Cheerfulness is the best promoter
Of health in each human being.
It's as friendly to the mind
As to the body – It's freeing!

Cheerfulness is a virtue;
It is a sign of wisdom.
Look for happy endings,
And you will rule your kingdom.

COURTESY

Schoepenhauer, now there's a name!
What a remarkable man was he!
Philosopher, thinker, problem solver –
His openness was his key.

He made a statement that's often quoted
About courtesy opening hearts,
How courtesy brings out the best in folks
And moves them to do their parts.

"By being polite and friendly you can
Make people obliging," said he.
It's really a more formal way to say:
Treat all people with courtesy.

You don't crush hearts – they are opened from within.
They respond more to kindness than force.
Graciousness guides those hinges wide open.
It's an attitude of love, of course.

Like responds to like, it's said.
We are treated the way we treat others.
Live as though all the people you meet
Are your sisters and your brothers.

Your lives will expand as you live your days.
Your fears will disappear, too.
Your heart will fill to overflowing
With everything you do.

GETTING ALONG

Since life is a mixture of good days and bad,
Of victory and defeat – give and take,
Getting along with your fellow man
Is not always a 'piece of cake.'

There are a few thoughts about getting along
That I'd like to pass on, if I can...
They're not always easy to implement,
But useful to every woman and man.

He who loses his temper usually loses. That's all.
There's nothing more to say about that.
And buck–passing acts as a boomerang. See?
It all comes back tit–for–tat.

Carrying tales of gossip, or carrying a chip
On your shoulder is not a good way
To get along with your fellow man –
And grumbling doesn't ever pay.

We are all human, and you can help
To make others feel better by seeing
Something good about them, then letting them know
They're special just for their 'being.'

Listening is often more important than talking –
A good blend of both is ideal.
And getting out and greeting the world
Is the first step to that great way to feel.

WALK ABOUT
(to a Johnny Cash beat and a bass guitar)

I don't want to be together; I don't want to be apart.
I don't want the stormy weather; I don't want to break your heart.
I don't want to sign a contract; I don't want to sleep alone.
I don't want to be so abstract; I don't want to just intone.

I just want some peace and quiet.
I just want to sort it out.
I just want to dare to try it.
I just want to walk about.

I don't want to be a "loser;" I'm afraid to "go for broke."
I don't want to be a "user;" I'm afraid it might provoke.
I don't know if I can make it; I'm afraid to really try.
I don't want to be a misfit; I'm afraid I'm going to cry.

I just want some peace and quiet.
I just want to sort it out.
I just want to dare to try it.
I just want to walk about.

I'm afraid to take the next step; I just want to greet the day.
I'm afraid to leave the doorstep; I just want to find my way.
I'm afraid I'll lose the prospect; I just want to learn to dance.
I'm afraid to gain my respect; I just guess I'll take the chance.

I just want some peace and quiet.
I just want to sort it out.
I just want to dare to try it.
I just want to walk about.

I just want to be a part of; I just want to lose my fear.
I just want to have that self-love; I just want to see things "clear."
I just want to win my races; I just want to do my best.
I just want to use the spaces; I just want to get some rest.

I just want some peace and quiet.
I just want to sort it out.
I just want to dare to try it.
I just want to walk about.

IN MY SOLITUDE

Solitude, Solo, Alone – but not lonely.
Friendship with self – by myself – only.
Time to listen to inner thoughts
Without the stigma of 'shoulds' or 'oughts.'
No fear of facing the stranger within;
And meeting me, my best friend, to rejoice in.

Solitude's a friend, not an enemy, not a foe.
Being alone is a way to know
Who that wonderful person is I hide –
The one I keep a secret inside.
I want to see me bared, unfurled,
Because if I know me, I'll know the world.

LIFE'S LESSONS

WORDS

If you use your words as a sword
You can always expect a duel;
And the louder the volume of the words in use
The more likely you'll play the fool.

Because arguing does to the spirit, my dears,
What disease can do to the body.
And an unhealthy spirit can give you what?
A life that's bound to be shoddy.

The greater number of words you use,
The less likely they are to be heard.
The greatest amount of impact comes
From carefully choosing each word.

Words are where most fights begin
Over when, wherefore or whether –
My advice is this: the brain and the mouth
Are meant to work together.

APPEARANCES

How do we seem to others?
Are we really ourselves...or who?
Do we come across as what we are inside,
Or as someone we never knew?

My guess is to others we are not ourselves,
But an actor in roles portraying –
A performer who's cast for an undefined part,
A part we don't know that we're playing.

The only issue we have to consider
Is whether or not we agree
To accept the roles that others assign us,
Or not be bothered, and live carefree.

ENDS & MEANS

Goals are set with hopes of attainment,
And to those ends we strive.
The way we strive is important here,
To the quality of how we survive.

The end can never justify the means,
For the simple and obvious explanation:
That the means employed determine the nature
Of the ends produced... its final manifestation.

MAKE YOUR OWN MISTAKES

Whatever you do, wherever you go,
Make sure it's a result of your choice.
When the static gets loud around your ears
Listen closely to your inner voice.

A misguided sense of obligation or duty
Can send you on a dead-end trail.
If you follow only your own compass and map
You will find you cannot fail.

Forgive yourself for wrong paths taken,
Perfection belongs to only a few.
Sometimes you need to be pushed to the brink
To know your life belongs to you.

LESSONS LEARNED

Everyone makes mistakes,
Though we try to do our best.
The ancients would only say:
"Errare humanum est."*

But there are people in this world
Who would comment when we blunder,
Who let us know we've goofed.
Here's a way to steal their thunder.

Acknowledge you've made a mistake.
(You're very human throughout.)
Just smile and politely say,
"Thanks for pointing that out."

Then use that information
To make changes, and enhance
Your happiness and success.
It is your second chance.

*It is human to err.

SECRETS OF LEADERSHIP

The secrets of becoming a good leader
Are many, and I won't pretend
To know them all, but here is one
I pass on to you as a friend.

When doing a job or a project
There's probably a right way... or wrong,
Whether you're planting a garden or an idea,
Playing baseball, or singing a song.

Don't think, "How can I do this differently?"
Or, "What is a better way?"
Think about how the job should be done, and
You will keep mediocrity at bay.

SELF HELP

Self help can be
Compared, you see,
To the likes of pumping iron.
Except it's space
Is in another place...
A less physical environ.

Manipulating weights
In pounds of eights
Builds physical strength in you.
And manipulating thoughts,
And getting rid of the 'nots'
Builds a new mental point of view.

TRY... OR DO?

Trying is trying, and tiring, too.
There is no trying! Just do!

AUTHENTICITY

If you accept your thoughts as facts
Then your road of discovery is blocked.
You assume you already know everything,
And your mind will, sadly, be locked.

You must be willing to challenge all aspects
Of your life, and its contents, it's true;
Including the reality you may be reaching
For things that aren't right for you.

There are no accidents in this life.
Of course, you knew that in advance.
So live your life with intention, because
Authenticity does not exist in a life left to chance.

KNOW-IT-ALLS

A person who claims to know it all
Is easy to spot in a crowd.
He's usually speaking in a tone of voice
With the volume incredibly loud.

A know-it-all can go on for hours
And imagines he does enthrall.
There are none more ignorant than those
Who think they know it all.

An expression I heard describing these types
(They're more than I care to handle!)
Is: People who think they're the whole ball of wax
Don't make a very good candle.

DECISION

Each day you are faced, sometimes thousands of times,
With the need to make a decision.
They're not always easy ones. So much is at stake!
You want to make them with precision.

The fate of life begins with choice,
Or so I've heard it said.
And you call the turns that determine your path.
You're responsible – A to Zed.

"Make decisions, make them as wisely as you can –
But make them," is the best advice I know.
And it's better to make a bad one now and then
Than to sit in indecisive woe.

Weigh the pros and cons, or get the expert's point of view,
But reserve your right to decide.
Your life is exactly what you make of it,
And the fence won't give you much of a ride.

Jump right in and stand up to life.
Don't let the winds blow you about.
Some wrong moves can happen till you finish refining,
But that's better than remaining in doubt.

FEAR AS MOTIVATOR

Fear can well up for all kinds of reasons.
It may even depend on the winds of the seasons.
Fear of death, fear of life, fear of failure or success –
You must be aware... and assess and address.

Replace the fear with the outcome you desire.
Think carefully about what you want and admire.
A positive result, not the negative mess –
Stay optimistic about it, lest you digress.

Running toward something that you desire
Is a healthier and much happier way to aspire
To what you want in life; not its reverse.
(Following what you don't want is most perverse!)

Running from fear only strengthens its hold;
To decide not to run is a step quite bold,
But worth the move to a life filled with love.
(An answer to the prayers you sent above.)

PERFECTION

Perfection is a goal to keep in mind
When performing a task of any kind.
Don't be disturbed if you fall short...
Pursuing perfection is an undefined sport.

There are many synonyms for the concept...
'Flawless,' 'ideal,' 'quintessential,' you accept.
In the world where it's rare to find perfection.
It seems necessary to make a correction.

But try, we do, to achieve the state;
Sometimes your efforts may frustrate.
Strive you must to reach your goal
(Trying, it seems, is an admirable role.)

Not much is perfect, that you know,
But striving for it brings you back tomorrow.
Undaunted you try, even if you're off a bit.
Your life will be better when trying becomes habit.

BATTLE YOUR DEMONS

To battle a demon is to embrace it.
To face it and stand your ground.
With clarity of vision and a humble heart
Respect its power profound.

To run from a demon is as effective
As running from a dog that is mad.
It beckons the chase, and sooner or later
You'll end up incredibly sad.

Whatever you resist you can be sure
It persists to torture and haunt.
Demons are the devilish agents of change.
You must face them as they taunt.

They throw down a gauntlet that awakens
The warrior within you to a duel.
A demon's job is to reduce your very being
Unless you face it – and rule.

Imagine yourself with a very bright light
Shining in the face of your demon.
How does it react when you stand your ground?
It leaves; You become a free man or woman.

THE REASONABLE MAN
(or Woman)

The reasonable man adapts himself
To the world in which he lives.
It seems a very logical move –
He gets just what he gives.

But the unreasonable man persists
In changing the world around him
To his needs; and when he does,
He can no longer be victim.

It's most ideal. It's liberating
To aim for one's desires –
To pinpoint need, and then work hard –
And watch as it transpires.

It's not the reasonable man to whom
Our plaudits we address.
It's the unreasonable one, there is no doubt,
Who's responsible for all progress!

PROBLEMS AS OPPORTUNITIES

Of all the wisdom on the subject of problems
I think I like Albert Einstein's the best!
His words cause one to pause and ponder,
And are not too difficult to digest.

"It's not that I'm so smart," he said,
"but I stay with problems longer."
A modest man, by reputation,
Which make his words ring stronger.

Many famous people become famous because
They overcame problems with new stratagems.
We are constantly faced with great opportunities,
Brilliantly disguised as insoluble problems.

Look at each of your problems as a gift...
A gift that when solved will let you know
That life is a series of new ideas to digest;
To incorporate into your being... and to grow.

KEEP THE END IN MIND

Completed goals bring on a sadness,
A letdown of varying degrees.
Before the job's done, there's something in the air,
A murmur, if you please.

It's energy at work in a positive direction
That creates a life of its own.
The joy that is gleaned is beyond description,
The joy of usefulness is well known.

It's good to have an end in mind
As you work toward your goal.
But in the end, it's the journey that matters
And how well you nurtured your soul.

It's not so much **what** you are doing,
As long as it is your bent;
It's **that** you're doing that matters most,
And that you continue to invent.

VISION

The most pathetic person in the world
Is someone with sight, but no vision.
He can see where he's walking, to be sure,
But his soul may be on course for collision.

As an example, many eyes walk through a meadow,
But few see the flowers blooming in it.
Perhaps they're looking for a path or a way...
And miss something that is quite exquisite.

What touches your soul is not the end gain,
But what your senses impart.
Your visions will become clear only when
You can look into your own heart.

Who looks only outside is dreaming his life
Not knowing the magic within.
Who looks inside awakens to it all,
And lives a life quite genuine.

ANGER DOES NOT DIMINISH LOVE

Anger and love are not mutually exclusive.
Anger does not have to mean "hate."
Anger, like any number of emotions,
Is just a brief pause in an angry state.

Don't give any special power to anger,
Like we do "sad" or "glad." It simply *is*, that's all.
The storm drifts over, and life goes on.
And the air is clearer after a lightning squall.

SEEING IS BELIEVING

'Looking' and 'seeing' use two different sets
Of equipment you have within.
'Looking' and 'seeing' are but qualities of
Your experience, or where you have been.

Some people respond, 'I see,' when they mean
'I have not the foggiest notion...'
And some see beyond words to the depths of their souls,
To the bottom of the deepest ocean.

You can teach yourself to look in depth
As a means to watch your life unfold.
Never turn your back on reality, my dears;
It surrounds you. It's there to behold.

When you think you can 'see,' look again and again.
Don't hesitate. Don't blink. Look again.
What you see may not be what you thought it was,
But be grateful for the knowledge you attain.

HONESTY

Pretense doesn't make sense.
It requires such effort
To maintain what isn't really true.
It's make-believe, play-acting and sham,
And affects everything you do.

The word without the heart is still unspoken;
It's feigned, it's pie-in-the-sky.
The deed without the doer remains undone;
It's 'acted,' and is a lie.

Saying and doing only what you think
That others would expect from you
Without searching your heart and inner soul
Is a sin. You know it, too.

Honesty must begin, like everything else,
With yourselves, with hearts so pure
That others can trust what you say and do.
The truth will always endure.

You're happiest when your conscience is clear,
When you've been honest about everything –
With yourselves and others (there is no difference).
Honesty to all you must bring.

It's so important to stay on the right track
In pursuing your long-range goals.
Stay honest with yourselves, and stay true,
And you'll have attained peaceful souls.

POSITIVE THOUGHTS

"As a man thinketh, so he is,"
Was said in wisdom long ago.
So it would follow, would it not,
That thinking 'positive' is the way to go?

We tend to become exactly the person
The thoughts in our head move us to be.
To find greater peace and happiness here,
The first step is thinking – positively.

LIFE'S GIFTS

CHILDREN OF THE LIGHT

There are those souls who bring the light,
Who spill it out for all to share,
And with a joy that does excite
They show the world that they do care.
It is so very bright.

In this sharing, love does pervade
Into their lives and cycles 'round;
And as this light is outward played
The love is also inward bound.
It is an awesome trade.

You are a soul whose light is shared.
It comes from deep within your heart.
It's best because it is not spared,
Because it's total, not just part.
And I am glad you've dared.

Author's Note:

Of all the poems I have written to and about my children, this one is my favorite.

The Greek Muse Erato was present the evening I put ink to paper to write *Children of the Light* and I shall never forget the feeling of focus and attention as the words spilled out onto the page.

Not a word has been changed in this poem from the night it was written. I believe that my children truly are *Children of the Light*, and everything I am as a mother I owe to them.

It is "an awesome trade."

– KCE

BELIEVE IN YOUR DREAMS

Let go of all your old beliefs
Of what you can and cannot do.
Remember, they are self-imposed,
And come from somewhere inside you!

Imagine yourself with canvas and paints;
And then with your phantasmic brush,
Paint a picture of what you would do
To bring joy to our world in a rush.

Once defined, this picture – fine and noble –
Requires only one thing in its hue:
A belief so strong in your "I can do it,"
Then action from an empowered you.

Open your heart and mind to the fire
Of creativity, love and animations.
Let go of old lies you've been telling yourself.
Let go of all self-imposed limitations.

FOOD FOR THOUGHT

One word, wrongly spoken, can take on a life
Of its own, and we helplessly stand by
As it runs its course, whatever that is.
You see the devastation, and you cry.

Your words can be soft or kind as you speak,
Or they can be harsh as they enter a fray.
Season your words with tenderness, for
You may have to eat them some day.

Words have power to exalt or deplete...
They're more powerful than you may think.
Your words are written on another's heart.
They're written in indelible ink.

Wrong words can spoil a meal or a snack,
Or whatever you have on your 'plate.'
We'd be better off if we worried more
About what we said than what we ate.

BRAVERY

It requires a lot of bravery to break new ground,
To do something no one else around is doing;
To escape from old ideas, once sound
And find something new that's worth pursuing.
The chance of success is, indeed, profound.

Bravery is knowing you are afraid,
But aiming for and pursuing your goal, anyway.
Bravery is contagious – and necessary in your crusade
It will convince others to help, I daresay.
Your bravery is powerful to persuade.

Stand up to your fears, look them in the face.
Be vulnerable and truthful and honest when you do.
Healthy fears are normal, and quite commonplace.
Overcoming them gives you a chance to continue,
And reach the success you were meant to embrace.

USEFULNESS

To be truly useful is to be fulfilled.
So, study a thing and become fully skilled.
With each mark of success you're bound to be thrilled.
You'll walk even taller as your praises are trilled.

Success comes to those who are self-willed.
Your attitude about work becomes instilled
When into your life good habits are drilled.
All of your concerns will likely be stilled.

MEMORY

The art of memory is seeking impressions
Which enrich your life as you grow.
Tomorrow's memory comes from today's expressions.
You reap, my dears, what you sow.

Your memory builds your personality;
Your personality builds your character: it follows.
Your character then determines your destiny;
A life with more peaks than hollows.

Memory is a gallery in which you collect beauty –
The world's wonders are yours to behold!
You 'own' the things you see, and more;
Memory's treasures surpass those of gold.

Memory is a mental bank account
From which you draw courage and hope,
And from what you've deposited as you have lived,
Your 'balance' will remain large in scope.

Memory is your link with the past centuries.
Remembrances are passed on to you.
It's a precious legacy you've inherited,
Giving continuity to all that you do.

Memory's a form of immortality
Because those you remember never die.
They continue to walk and talk with you.
Memory keeps them always near by.

The quality of your life will determine the memories
That others will have of you.
Stay positive and helpful, and do enjoy
All that you think and do.

PEACE OF MIND

Be content with what you have;
Rejoice in the way things are.
Then, if changes need to be made...
With peace of mind; you'll go far.

When you realize there is nothing lacking,
The whole world belongs to you.
Your needs, your wants, are gone in a flash.
You have a different point of view.

Your treasure trove is in yourself.
It contains all you'll ever need.
You're remarkable, you can do anything!
In every venture you will succeed.

COURAGE

Life shrinks or expands in proportion to one's courage.
Don't waste your time striving for someone else's dreams.
Have the courage to follow your own heart and intuition.
No one else's life is as wonderful as it seems.

Efforts and courage require purpose and direction.
Failure is not fatal, and success is never the end.
Dreams are not pursued because of lack of courage.
Courage is grace under pressure. Do you comprehend?

Creativity requires the courage to let go of certainties,
To release the familiar and to embrace what you find.
You'll never do anything in this world without courage.
Next to honor, it's the greatest quality of the mind.

The opposite for courage is surely not cowardice.
'Conformity' is the opposite, and not good for one's health.
One person with courage is a decided majority.
The most courageous act is to think for yourself.

COMPASSION

"Love and compassion are necessities.
Without them, humanity cannot survive."
(So said the Dalai Lama.)
And, with them, humanity can thrive.

Albert Schweitzer weighed in on the subject
Saying, "The purpose of life is to serve,
And to show compassion and the will
To help others" – not just observe.

Lao Tzu, the father of Taoism,
Said he had three things to teach:
Simplicity, patience and compassion.
(Your greatest treasure, I beseech!)

Compassion binds us one to another,
As we humans go along our way.
We've learned how to turn what we share
Into hope for the future each day.

A CLOSING THOUGHT

POETRY

It's the revelation
Of a sensation
That the poet
(Wouldn't you know it)
Believes to be
Felt only interiorly
And personal to
The writer who
... writes it.

It's the interpretation
Of a sensation
That was fueled by
A poet's sigh
And believed to be
Shared mutually
And personal to
The lucky one who
... reads it.

About the authoR

Kathryn Carole Ellison is a former newspaper columnist
and journalist and, of course, a poet.

She lives near her children and stepchildren and their families in the
Pacific Northwest, and spends winters in the sunshine of Arizona.

You might find her on the golf course with friends, river rafting,
writing poems... or at the opera.

Late bloomeR

Our culture honors youth with all
It's unbridled effervescence.
We older ones sit back and nod
As if in acquiescence.

And when our confidence really gels
In early convalescence...
"We can't be getting old!" we cry,
"We're still struggling with adolescence!"

Acknowledgments

I have many people to thank...

First of all, my children Jon and Nicole LaFollette, for inspiring the writing of these poems in the first place. And for encouraging me to continue my writing, even though their wisdom and compassion surpass mine.

My wonderful stepchildren, Debbie and John Bacon, Jeff and Sandy Ellison, and Tom and Sue Ellison, who, with their children and grandchildren, continue to be a major part of my life and are loved deeply by me. These poems are for you, too.

Eva LaFollette, the dearest daughter-in-law one could ever wish for... and one of my dearest friends. Your encouragement and interest are so appreciated.

My good friends who have received a poem or two of mine in their Christmas cards these many years, for complimenting me on the messages in my poems. Your encouragement kept me writing.

To Kim Kiyosaki who introduced me to the right person to get the publishing process underway... that person being Mona Gambetta with Brisance Books Group who has the experience and know-how to make these books happen.

And finally, to John Laughlin, a fellow traveler in life, who encourages me every day in the writing and publishing process. John, I love having you in my cheering section!

OTHER BOOKS
by Kathryn Carole Ellison

CELEBRATIONS

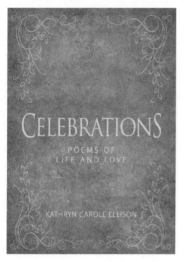

HEARTSTRINGS